POLLUTION AND WASTE

ROSIE HARLOW & SALLY MORGAN

KING*f*ISHER

NEW YORK

KINGFISHER
Larousse Kingfisher Chambers Inc.
95 Madison Avenue
New York, New York 10016
First Published in 1995
10 9 8 7 6 5 4 3 (PB)

3TR/0499/WKT/HBM/128KMA

10 9 8 7 6 5 4 3 2 1 (RLB)

LIBRARY OF CONGRESS CATALOGING-IN-
PUBLICATION DATA
Harlow, Rosie.
Pollutin and waste/Rosie Harlow,
Sally Morgan.—1st American ed.
p. cm. (Young discoverers)
Includes bibliographical references
and index.
1. Pollution—Juvenile literature.
[1. Pollution.] I. Morgan, Sally. II. Title.
III. Series.
TD176.H37 1995 363. 73—dc20
95-6369 CIP AC

ISBN 1-85697-613-0 (PB)
ISBN 1-85697-614-9 (RLB)

Editor: Jilly MacLeod
Designer: Ben White
Art editor: Val Wright
Photo research: Elaine Willis
Cover design: John Jamieson and
    Shaun Barlow
Illustrations: Julian Baker p. 19, 22 (top
    and right), 24-25, 26 (top), 30 (top);
    Peter Bull p. 4, 5 (inset), 6-7, 9, 10
    (top), 12, 18; Deborah Kindred p. 5,
    26 (bot.), 27; Janos Marffy p. 11 (bot.),
    15 (left), 16 (top), 20 (top), 23, 28-29,
    30 (bot.), 31; Mike Saunders p. 8, 10
    (bot.), 11 (top), 13, 14, 15 (right),
    16-17, 20 (bot.), 21; Dan Wright
    p. 22 (left)
Photographs: Ecoscene p. 4 (J. Millership),
    9 (Hibbert), 13, 15, 17 (N. Hawkes),
    25 (Harwood), 27 (Jones), 31 (Winkley);
    Robert Harding Picture Library p. 7, 19;
    NHPA p. 21 (D. Woodfall); Science
    Photo Library p. 12 (M. Bond)

Printed in Hong Kong

About This Book

This book looks at pollution and waste and explains how we are damaging our environment by creating too much of it. It suggests lots of experiments and things to look out for, as well as ways we can help to make our world a cleaner and safer place.

You should be able to find nearly everything you need for the experiments in and around your home. Be sure to ask an adult to help you with the experiment on page 7—it is dangerous to light a candle on your own.

Activity Hints
• Before you begin an experiment, read through the instructions carefully and collect all the things you need.
• When you have finished, clear everything away, especially sharp scissors, and wash your hands.
• Start a special notebook so you can keep a record of what you do in each experiment and the things you find out.

Contents

What is Pollution?

Every day we pour harmful substances such as poisonous gases, chemicals, and garbage, into our environment. Harmful substances that damage the environment are called pollution. Most pollution comes from factories and transportation, but as you will see, we all contribute to it in some way. It is difficult to stop pollution, but it must be done before we cause too much damage.

When rocks are dug up from quarries to make new roads and buildings, ugly holes are left that spoil the beauty of the countryside. Scars in the landscape are a form of visual pollution.

Do it yourself

Make some simple pollution testers.

To test rain for pollution, line a funnel with a coffee filter. Put the funnel in a jar and place your tester outside in the rain. Check the filter paper after an hour to see how dirty it is. Take a closer look through a magnifying glass.

On a dry day, smear Vaseline inside three metal lids. Place one lid inside your home, one on the street, and one in the park. After a day, compare them to see how much dirt has collected. Which place is dirtiest?

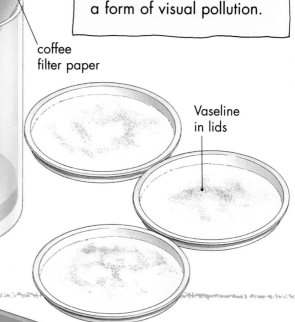

rainwater

coffee filter paper

Vaseline in lids

magnifying glass

air transportation

spraying fertilizer

Poisonous gases from factories and transportation pollute the air. Garbage, sewage, and chemicals poured into rivers and oceans pollute our water. Mining for rock, metals, and coal causes water and visual pollution. Spraying pesticides and fertilizers pollutes the land.

Eye-Spy

Do a pollution survey by seeing how much litter, noise, and smelly fumes there are in your street. Write down your results on a chart. Then try the park, the main street, and your backyard. Which place is the most polluted?

factory fumes

road transportation

coal mine

Pollution happens in your home and your street. Garbage spills from garbage cans and cars pump out exhaust fumes.

car exhaust fumes

garbage

5

Dirty Air

Every minute of every day we breathe in air. Clean air is essential for life. It is a mixture of gases, mainly oxygen and nitrogen, with small amounts of carbon dioxide, plus water. Air has no color or smell, except when it is polluted. Dirty air can affect the health of humans, animals, and plants and can even damage buildings. Industry and transportation produce almost all the pollution in our air, releasing millions of tons of harmful gases and soot into the environment each year.

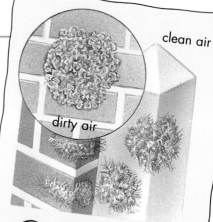

clean air

dirty air

👁 Eye-Spy

Lichens are crispy plantlike growths found on trees, rocks, and buildings. You can test for air pollution by finding out which types grow near your home. Thick, hairy lichens only grow in clean air. Flat lichens (inset) can grow in dirty air.

The Air Cycle

All the oxygen in our air comes from trees and other plants. They take carbon dioxide from the air and use it to make food, giving off oxygen as they do so. Animals breathe in the oxygen and release carbon dioxide, which the plants use to make more food. But factories and homes burn fuels for heat, which use up oxygen and release too much carbon dioxide and other poisonous gases into the air.

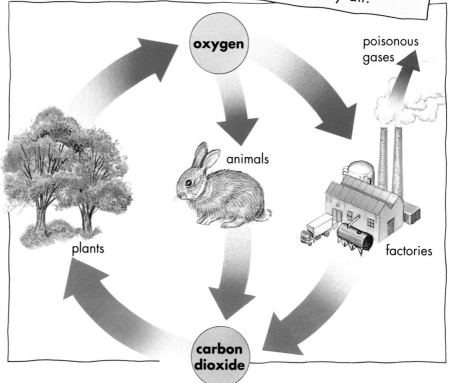

oxygen

poisonous gases

animals

plants

factories

carbon dioxide

Do it yourself

Burning coal to make electricity, gasoline to power cars, or gas for heating pollutes the air. Ask an adult to help you see how much dirt is made, even when a candle burns.

Simply light a candle and bring a heat-proof dish down over the yellow part of the flame for 30 seconds. Move the dish from side to side as you do so. Now look at the underside of your dish.

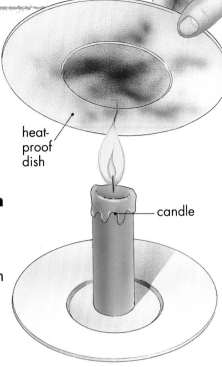

heat-proof dish

candle

How It Works

The black sooty carbon that collects on the underside of the dish is produced when the wax of the candle burns. This carbon usually goes up into the air so you do not see it. Gases are also produced, but you don't see them either.

Polluting Our Body

Ask someone who smokes to take a puff from a cigarette without inhaling, then to breathe the smoke out through a white tissue. The black mark on the tissue is a substance called "tar" which is produced as the tobacco burns. This normally collects in a layer inside the smoker's lungs.

Factory chimneys pump out dirty fumes that are carried far away by the wind.

7

Rain That Burns

Sometimes rain contains chemicals called acids that can harm wildlife and damage buildings. Acids cause so much harm because they can "burn" into materials. Acid rain forms when sulfur dioxide and nitrogen dioxide, produced by burning fuel, are released into the air. The two gases mix with water to form a weak acid, which falls as rain. Winds may carry the rain far away from the source of pollution. Millions of trees in North America and Europe are now dying from acid rain damage.

Salmon at Risk

Salmon are the first fish to be affected by acid rain. The acid causes aluminum to be washed from the soil into rivers and lakes where it affects the fish's gills.

The gases that cause acid rain are released by power plants, factories, and transportation. Acid rain falls to the ground and is taken up by tree roots, eventually causing the trees to die. The acid rain may also drain into lakes and rivers.

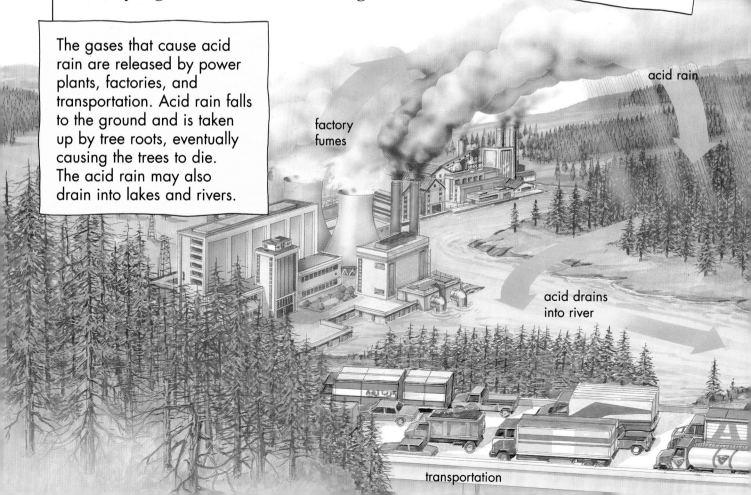

acid rain

factory fumes

acid drains into river

transportation

Do it yourself

See how acids can damage plants.

Dip some leaves in a small jar of vinegar and then leave them with their stalks in the vinegar for a few days.

How It Works

Vinegar is a weak kind of acid. The acid damages the leaf from both the inside and the outside, so the leaf soon goes brown and dies.

leaves damaged by acid

vinegar

healthy tree

damaged tree

 Eye-Spy

Look around at the trees where you live—in your yard, park, or street. Can you see any signs of damage by acid rain? This picture shows you what to look for.

This stone figure (above) has been damaged by acid rain, making it difficult to see the features of the head and body.

More Things To Try

This experiment shows how quickly an acid can eat into rocks. Chalk is used because it is similar to the kinds of rock used on buildings, such as sandstone and limestone, only it is softer. Just put a piece of chalk into a dish of vinegar and watch what happens. Vinegar is stronger than acid rain, so it eats away the chalk much faster than acid rain would.

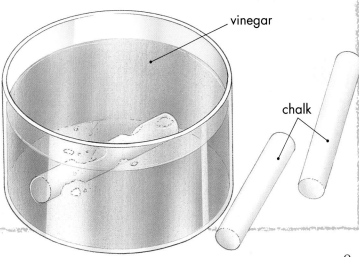

vinegar

chalk

9

Cleaning Up Our Act

Probably the biggest causes of air pollution are oil, gas, and coal. If we burned fewer of these fuels (called fossil fuels) then we would reduce pollution. There are many laws that control the amount of pollution a factory or car can produce. But it would be better still if we used alternative, cleaner sources of energy, such as solar, wind, or water power. As well as causing less pollution, these kinds of energy are renewable—that is, they will not run out. Fossil fuels, on the other hand, are non-renewable and will run out one day.

Switch Off Engines

Cars stuck in traffic jams pump out a lot of air pollution. This sign asks drivers to turn off their car engine while they wait at traffic lights, in order to cut down air pollution.

Alternative Energy

We can make electricity using any one of these alternative sources of energy. Hydroelectric dams built across fast-flowing rivers use the power of water to make electricity. Hot rocks deep in the ground can be used to heat water. This is called geothermal power. Many places in the world have strong winds that can be used to turn the blades of wind generators. And energy from the Sun can be trapped using solar panels.

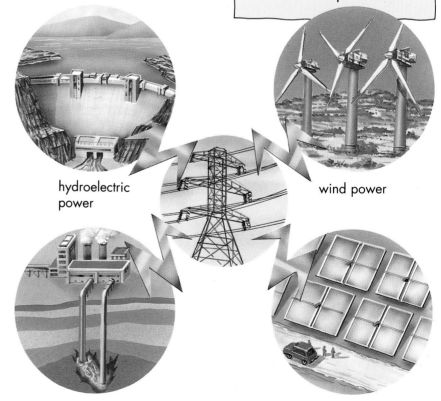

hydroelectric power

wind power

geothermal power

solar power

How Can We Help?

We can help to reduce air pollution by using less electricity and gasoline.

- Walk or use public transportation, not a car.
- Give friends a lift on regular journeys.
- Turn off lights, the TV, and other electrical items when they are not in use.
- Use low-energy light bulbs at home.

Powering Cars

In the future, electric cars will be a common sight on our roads. However, the batteries of an electric car have to be "recharged" regularly to replace the energy that has been used up. The car batteries could be recharged using solar energy, which would mean little pollution and less cost.

electric car

battery recharger

solar panels

Do it yourself

The Sun's heat energy is absorbed, or taken up, by some colors and reflected by others. Find out which color absorbs the most heat and would be best for heating water in a solar panel.

1. Cut pieces of cardboard about 4 inches square. Make each one a different color—black, white, yellow, red, or green. Lay the cards out in the Sun and feel them as they warm up. Which one warms up the quickest?

2. Put an ice cube on each piece of card. Which one melts the quickest and which one melts the slowest?

How It Works

Black is best at absorbing heat from the Sun, so the black card warms up fastest. White reflects the Sun's heat so the white card takes longest. The other colors only absorb some of the heat. A black material is used in solar panels to trap the Sun's heat.

New Forms of Power

Scientists are always trying to find new sources of energy that will not cause pollution. One experiment being carried out in Loch Ness, in Scotland, uses floating bags, called clams, to trap the power of the waves and make electricity for local homes. The clams shown here are only one-fourteenth of their full size. Maybe in the future we will be using clams to supply homes across the world with electricity.

Do it yourself

Use the power of the wind to spin this fun pinwheel.

1. Cut a piece of paper—6 inches square. Snip in toward the center from each corner as shown. Fold four opposite corners over to the center and glue them down, overlapping them slightly.

2. Thread a pin through the center of your wheel and push it into an eraser on top of a pencil. Now see how the wind can make it spin.

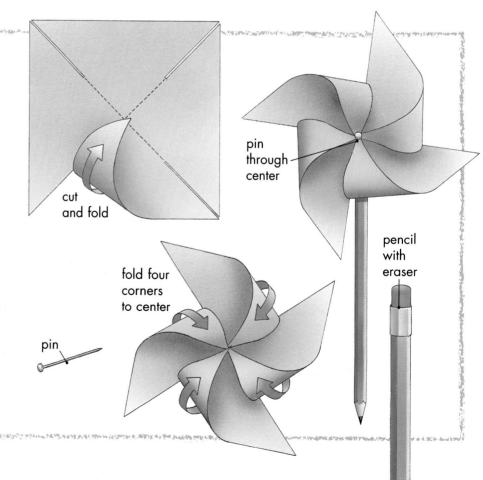

cut and fold

fold four corners to center

pin

pin through center

pencil with eraser

Holes in the Sky

The atmosphere is an envelope of air, 300 miles (500km) thick, that completely surrounds the Earth. About 15 miles (25km) up is a thin layer known as the ozone layer. Ozone is a special form of oxygen. It is very important because it protects the Earth against harmful "ultraviolet" rays from the Sun. But the ozone is being destroyed by chemicals called CFCs (chlorofluorocarbons) that have escaped into the atmosphere. The damage is worst over Antarctica, where the CFCs are eating a hole in the ozone layer.

Banned!

CFCs were used in fridges, aerosol cans, and types of packaging such as fast-food containers. Fortunately, they are now being banned from use.

Sun

CFCs moving upward from the Earth make the ozone layer over Antarctica very thin. This is called the ozone hole. Harmful ultraviolet light, most of which is usually blocked by the ozone layer, can get through the hole to reach the Earth's surface.

ultraviolet rays

CFCs move upward

Too much ultraviolet light is harmful because it can cause skin cancer. Sunbathers use sun cream to protect their skin.

Things Are Heating Up

The Earth's atmosphere acts like a blanket, trapping in heat and keeping the Earth warm. Without this blanket, the Earth would be frozen and lifeless. The heat is trapped by gases that act like the glass of a greenhouse, letting in the heat but preventing it from getting out again. The gases are known as greenhouse gases. Unfortunately, the amount of these gases in the atmosphere is increasing as a result of pollution. The gases are trapping more heat and the Earth is getting hotter.

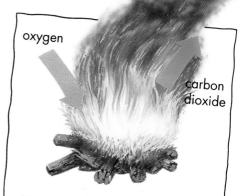

Burning Fuels

When we burn fuels such as coal, oil, and wood, oxygen is used up and carbon dioxide is released. Carbon dioxide is one of the greenhouse gases.

oxygen

carbon dioxide

Greenhouse Effect

When heat from the Sun hits the Earth, some of the heat is absorbed. This keeps the Earth and its atmosphere warm. Only a small amount of heat escapes back into space—most of it is trapped by the greenhouse gases. As the amount of greenhouse gases increases, the Earth gets warmer. This may affect the world's climate. Parts of the polar ice caps could melt, the level of the sea could rise, and low-lying countries might be flooded.

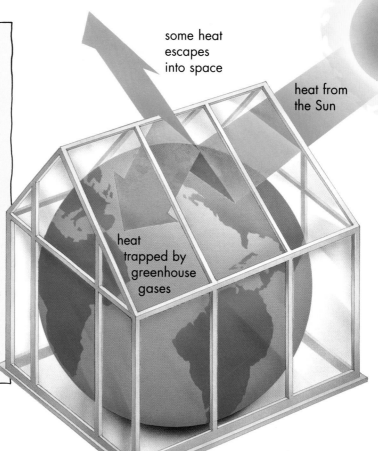

some heat escapes into space

heat from the Sun

heat trapped by greenhouse gases

Greenhouse Gases

Carbon dioxide is one of the most important greenhouse gases. But methane also adds to the effect. Cows produce methane, and as more people keep more cows, the level of methane is going up. CFCs are also greenhouse gases, so they too are helping to heat up the atmosphere.

Do it yourself

Do this test to see how the greenhouse effect works.

1. Lay a thermometer outside on a sunny day and read the temperature after five minutes.

2. Now put the thermometer inside a clear plastic bag. Puff out the bag with your hands to let lots of air inside, then close the opening and seal it with tape.

3. Leave the bag in the sun for five minutes and then read the temperature of the air inside the bag. Is it higher than your previous reading?

heat from the Sun

plastic bag

thermometer

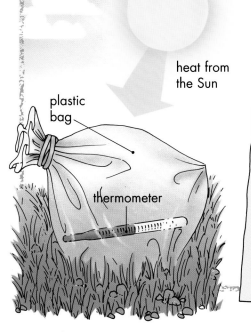

How It Works

The air inside the bag gets warmer than the air outside because the layer of plastic traps the Sun's heat inside. This is similar to the way greenhouse gases trap heat from the Sun inside the Earth's atmosphere, making it warmer.

Is Greenland Green?

Today, Greenland is covered in thick ice. But when it was named by the Vikings long ago it was much warmer and the land was green. Maybe it is normal to have warm periods, and we are worrying unnecessarily about the greenhouse effect.

Polluting Our Water

All animals and plants need a supply of clean water to survive. You may think we have plenty of water, but only a fraction of it is fresh water that we can use, and we are polluting this in the same way as we are damaging the atmosphere. When pollutants such as oil and chemical wastes are poured into water, they are soon carried away by the tides or by the flow of the river and are extremely difficult to remove. One of the most damaging forms of oil pollution in water comes from waste car oil that has been poured down the drain.

👁 Eye-Spy

Next time you go near a river or stream, look out for signs of pollution, such as detergents frothing up with foam, oil floating on the water, old tires, bottles and tin cans, or dead fish.

As a river winds its way to the sea, many different chemicals may enter its waters. Harmful chemicals may seep out of landfill sites (where garbage is buried). Pesticides and fertilizers may drain into it from farmland. And sewage from local towns may be poured in. In most countries, sewage now has to be treated before it is emptied into rivers.

landfill site

Rock-Pooling

Looking for animals and plants in rock pools on the beach is great fun. If you find lots of wildlife, you know you are looking at an unpolluted beach.

Banned!

In the past, many countries dumped poisonous wastes and sewage at sea. There are now international laws to stop this happening, and people have to find less harmful ways of getting rid of waste. Even so, some illegal dumping still goes on.

Factories produce a lot of dirty water, much of which ends up in nearby rivers.

Oil spills from ships and oil tankers at sea can cause terrible harm to wildlife.

factories

sewage

farming

oil spillage

Do it yourself

Do these simple tests to see how oil spills can be removed from water.

1. Fill a bowl with water and pour several drops of cooking oil into it. Watch how the oil floats to the surface in a blob.

2. Stir the oil around with a spoon handle. Try breaking it up and then joining it back together again.

3. Now dip a small piece of white paper into the water where the oil is lying. See how the oil disappears off the surface of the water and the paper gradually changes color.

4. Put a few more drops of cooking oil into the water. Then add a couple of drops of dishwashing detergent and see what happens.

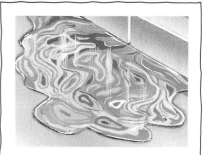

 Eye-Spy

Next time it rains, look at the side of the road for puddles with swirling colors of pink, purple, blue, and yellow. These mini oil slicks are made by car oil spreading out over the water's surface.

How It Works

Oil always floats on water. The paper absorbs the oil from the surface of the water, changing color as it does so. In the same way, when a tanker spills oil on the sea, layers of absorbent material are floated on the surface of the water to soak up the oil.

Detergents such as dishwashing liquid break up the blob of oil and spread it out in a thin layer over the surface of the water. Detergents can be used to clean up oil spills at sea. Unfortunately, they can also harm wildlife.

Down on the Farm

Farming has changed over the last 200 years. In the past, the fields were small and horses were used to pull machinery. Today, huge fields stretch as far as the eye can see, and powerful combine harvesters and tractors have taken over. Often the same crop is grown on the land for many years, and chemicals are used to increase the yield (output). This type of "intensive" farming can cause pollution and harm wildlife.

Chemical Sprays

Farmers spray fertilizers on their crops to help them grow fast, and pesticides to kill off wildlife that might damage them. But these chemicals cause pollution.

Many farm animals never see a field. They are kept crowded together in special barns. Their waste, called slurry, can pollute rivers, so it must be disposed of carefully.

In the 1930s, farms in the Midwest were hit by a long drought. With huge fields and so few trees, there was nothing to stop strong winds blowing away the dry soil. This created a vast dust bowl that could not be farmed.

Organic Farming

Although it does not produce as much food as intensive farming, organic farming is much better for the land. The fields are smaller and more trees are allowed to grow. Farmers do not use chemical sprays that cause pollution. And farm animals are free to roam.

Each year, organic farmers "rotate" their crops. That is, they change the crop grown in each field. This stops the buildup of pests and disease. They keep their soil healthy by mixing in lots of animal manure. As well as feeding the crops, the manure holds the soil together so it does not blow away. The animals are free-range, so they can wander in the fields instead of being kept in barns.

Intercropping

Sometimes organic farmers control pests and improve the yield by growing two different crops together in the same field. This method of farming is called intercropping.

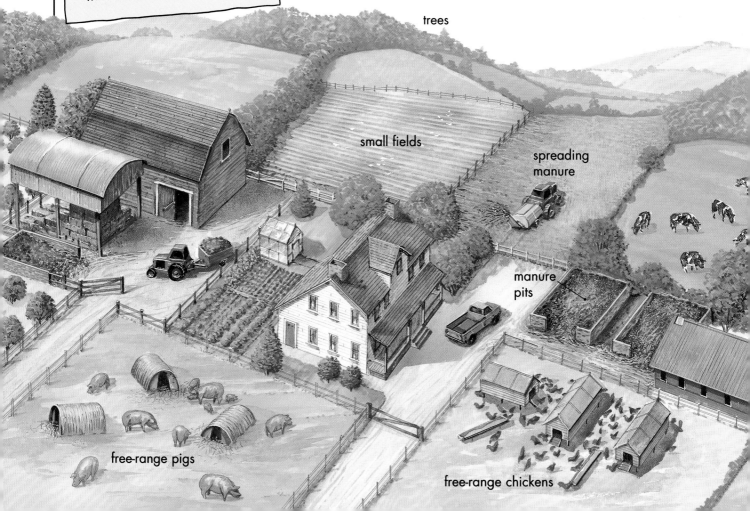

trees

small fields

spreading manure

manure pits

free-range pigs

free-range chickens

👁 Eye-Spy

Milk, eggs, meat, fruits, and vegetables can all be produced by organic farming methods. See how many different types of organic foods you can see in your local shops.

Making a Choice

Fruits and vegetables in shops often look perfect. This is because they have been sprayed with chemicals to kill any pests that might spoil their appearance.

Organically grown fruits and vegetables are not sprayed. They do not look as perfect but they taste just as good, if not better! Which type would you buy if you had a choice?

Organic farmers use natural fertilizers such as manure and compost to feed their crops. These are just as rich as chemical fertilizers, but they are not as polluting.

produce grown using chemical sprays

organically grown produce

Problems with Pests

Pests damage crops. A pest may be an animal that eats the crop, a fungus that causes disease, or a weed that competes with the crop for space, water, or food. Farmers may use a variety of different pesticides to kill pests—such as insecticides, fungicides, and herbicides. But most pesticides also kill other animals and plants, not just the pest. For example, an insecticide used to destroy aphids may also kill insects such as butterflies. Organic farmers have found other, less harmful methods of pest control.

Banned!

Some pesticides are so harmful that they have been banned from use. But it may take many years for them to break down and disappear completely.

What Went Wrong?

Cane toads were introduced to the sugarcane fields of Australia to control pests. But the toads ignored the pests and fed on other animals instead. Now these toads have become pests themselves.

crops

birds eat grubs

aphids feed on crops

hover fly grubs eat aphids

Organic farmers use natural predators to control pests. (A predator is an animal that feeds on other animals.) Aphids damage many crops. The grubs of

hover flies feed on aphids, so farmers attract hover flies by planting certain types of flowers close to the crops. The hover flies are then eaten by small birds.

Do it yourself

Do this experiment to see how easily chemicals are taken up by plants.

1. Pour water into a glass so it is about $\frac{1}{4}$ inch deep. Then add a similar amount of red or blue food coloring.

2. Cut the end off a stick of celery or a lettuce leaf and put it in the glass. Check every half hour to see how far the colored water has spread through the plant.

lettuce leaf

celery

food coloring

More Things To Try

Try making this unusual flower display. Put a few daisies in water mixed with different food colorings. Leave them to absorb the dyes, then arrange them in a small vase.

How It Works

Plants need water to live. They absorb water from the soil and draw it up through their stems to their leaves. The food coloring used in this experiment is drawn up into the plant along with the water, dyeing the plant an unusual color. In the same way, harmful chemicals in the soil can be drawn into the plants we eat.

Getting Rid of Waste

We produce more waste today than ever before, so it is important that we get rid of it safely, without harming the environment. People throw away ten times their own body weight in garbage every year. This is either buried in the ground or burned. Every day gallons of dirty water disappear down the drain. The water has to be treated before it can be pumped back into rivers and oceans. Industry also produces waste. This is usually dumped in a landfill, poured into rivers and seas, or burned.

Mountains of Litter

Litter is a form of waste. It gets everywhere, even on Mount Everest, where climbers drop their garbage on the mountainside.

Where It Comes From

Waste matter comes from many different sources. Factories produce liquid and solid wastes, as well as gases. Intensive animal farming produces slurry. And every home produces dirty water and sewage, along with household garbage.

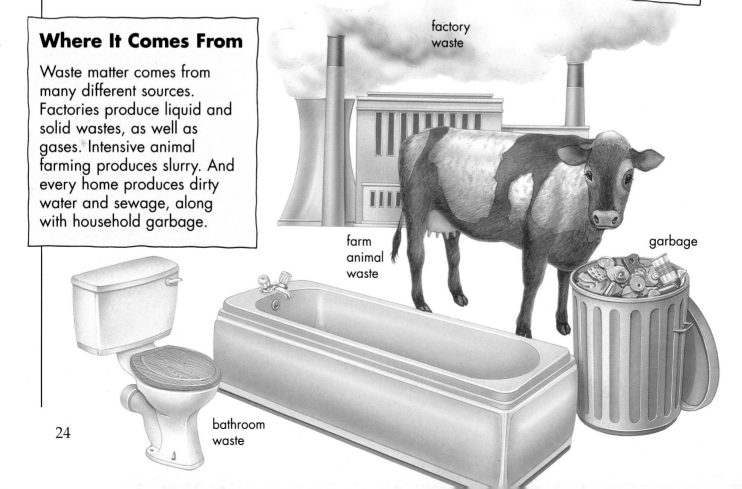

factory waste

farm animal waste

garbage

bathroom waste

24

Toxic (poisonous) industrial waste is difficult to get rid of safely. Some of it has to undergo special treatment before it can be put back into the environment. This can be very expensive.

Water pouring out of a waste pipe into a river is a common sight in many countries. This water often contains chemicals that can harm animals and plants.

Scoop the Poop!

Dog mess is a form of waste that can be very unpleasant. We can try to keep our parks and streets clean by using specially provided dog garbage cans.

Do it yourself

Organize a "litter blitz."

Litter is one of the most unnecessary forms of waste. It spoils our environment and harms wildlife. Get together with some friends and clean up your local street, park, school ground, or beach. Pick up all the litter you can find, put it in plastic garbage bags and throw it away properly. Be sure to wear gloves when handling litter.

How Can We Help?

Try to reduce litter and waste where you live.

- Don't drop litter.
- Make and display a poster in your window asking people to keep your neighborhood a "litter-free zone."
- Organize your friends and neighbors to do a litter blitz.
- Don't allow your dog to foul the sidewalks or local park. If it does, be sure to clear it up.

25

Too Much Noise

Modern towns and cities are very noisy places. There is a constant rumble from traffic, and the sound of machinery, alarms, and sirens fills the air. Noise is a form of pollution, too. Some people live near noisy places such as airports. They are deafened by the sound of airplanes as they take off and land. Other people have to work in noisy factories. Noise can damage your hearing, especially if you have to listen to something loud for a long time.

How Can We Help?

Try to keep the level of noise pollution down.

- Keep the volume of music and the television down at home so you don't disturb your family or neighbors.
- Don't play loud music or the radio outdoors where it could disturb other people.
- Don't slam doors.
- Don't thunder up or down stairs—try to walk quietly.

👁 Eye-Spy

Our world is so full of sound that we often "switch our ears off" so that we do not hear many familiar noises. Try taping some everyday noises around your home, then play them back to hear how noisy they really are.

The thunder of trucks, the blast of car horns, and the clamor of a drill all add to the din on a noisy street. Even loud music is a form of noise pollution!

What a Sight!

Every day, roads are built across unspoiled countryside. To build the roads, rocks are dug up from quarries which scar the landscape. Rows of ugly power lines carry electricity to all parts of the country, and new factories and landfills are built on sites that were once covered in grassland or woodland. All this spoils our countryside and is a form of visual (sight) pollution.

Attractive countryside can be spoiled by power lines, landfills, and new roads. Many shopping centers are built outside the cities, spoiling the land.

Sometimes we can restore spoiled land. This attractive park used to be a landfill site full of garbage. It has been covered with soil and planted with trees.

👁 Eye-Spy

Next time you take a car trip, look out for signs of visual pollution. What sort of things do you think spoil the scenery?

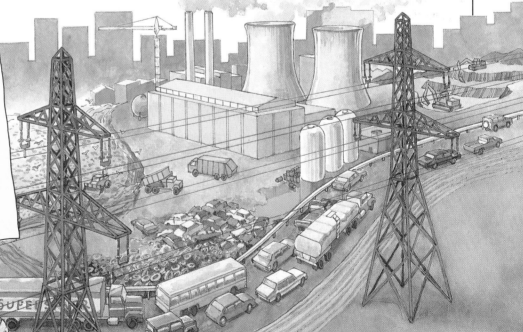

Pollution at Home

Many of the substances we use at home can cause pollution. Cleaners can be particularly harmful. One of the most polluting is bleach, which is used to kill germs. And detergents often contain chemicals called phosphates that can pollute local rivers and lakes. Artificial perfumes in furniture polishes and air fresheners pollute the air. Even medicines can be harmful if they get into the environment. To help reduce pollution, many household substances are now made to be "environmentally friendly."

Keeping Clean

Clean bodies are healthy, and to stay clean we use an array of shampoos, soaps, and deodorants. But the colors and perfumes often added to these products to make them feel good are not really necessary and can sometimes irritate the skin.

Here are just some of the harmful substances you may have at home. Read the labels on the cleaners to see if the ones you have are environmentally friendly.

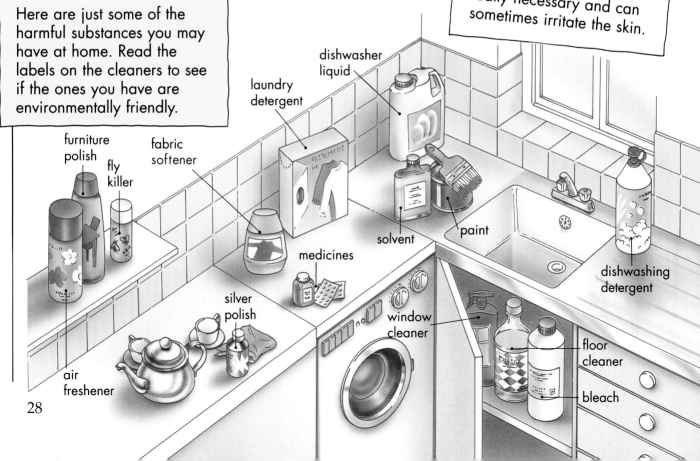

Do it yourself

Instead of using artificial air fresheners, make your bedroom smell sweet with these pretty pomanders.

1. Take an orange and tie a brightly colored ribbon around it. Finish off with a big bow on top. Cut the tails of the bow into a V-shape.

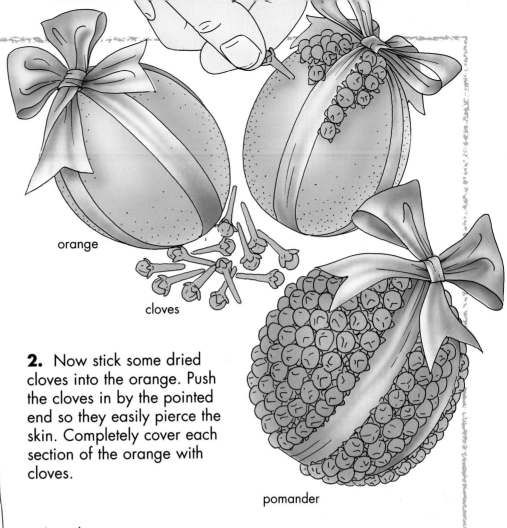

orange

cloves

pomander

2. Now stick some dried cloves into the orange. Push the cloves in by the pointed end so they easily pierce the skin. Completely cover each section of the orange with cloves.

More Things To Try

Another natural way to keep your room smelling sweet is to use potpourri. It is quite easy to make. You will need some dried lavender and dried purple and blue flowers such as larkspur, delphiniums, or statice. You can buy these in special shops that sell dried flowers and some department stores.

Put the flowers in a bowl with a pinch each of ground nutmeg, ginger, and cinnamon. Mix all together with your fingers and place in a plastic bag. Seal the bag and leave it in a dry dark place for six weeks. Now put your potpourri out in a pretty bowl.

potpourri

How Can We Help?

- Make sure the cleaners you buy are biodegradable. This means they will break down quickly and will not cause pollution.
- Take harmful substances such as old paints, batteries, medicines, and oil to your your local recycling center where they can be recycled or safely disposed of.

Recycle It!

Why throw something away if it could be recycled (reused) to make something new? It makes a lot of sense to recycle. The more we recycle, the less garbage ends up in landfill sites. Recycling also reduces the need for raw materials and saves energy. It is particularly important to recycle metals that are in limited supply, such as copper and lead. Nowadays, there are special recycling centers where you can take your garbage. When you use them, you are helping to reduce pollution.

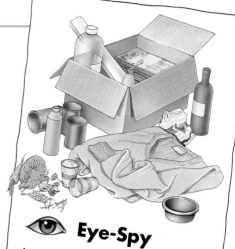

Eye-Spy

Look out for things at home that can be recycled. They include aluminum foil; tin cans; glass bottles; plastic bags, and bottles; newspapers; cardboard boxes; and old clothes.

Do it yourself

Make some recycled monster masks out of old newpapers and bits of garbage.

1. First, make the basic masks out of papier-mâché. Blow up a round balloon to use as a mold—this will give you two masks.

2. Mix up some thick paste from flour and water in a small bowl.

3. Tear some newspaper into strips about 1 inch wide. Coat a strip with paste using an old paintbrush, then paste it onto the balloon.

4. Cover the balloon with a layer of newspaper strips. Then add three more layers of newspaper in the same way. Leave the papier-mâché to dry for a day or two.

5. Pop the balloon and cut the papier-mâché model in half as shown, using a pair of scissors. Then cut holes for the eyes and mouth.

6. Give both your masks a coat of white paint, both inside and out. When this has dried, paint your masks a bright color.

Nearly every home has a bottle bank nearby, so there is no excuse for throwing away glass bottles. First the glass is collected, washed and crushed. Then it is melted and used to make new glass bottles. By recycling glass, fewer raw materials are needed and much less energy is used.

green plastic bottle strips

bottle tops

aluminum foil

cork

strands of yarn

foam packaging or paper

tissue paper strips

7. Decorate your masks with corks, bottle tops, foil, yarn, plastic bottles cut into strips, and tissue paper. Glue or tape the pieces in place.

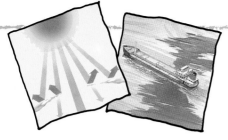

Index

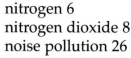